A Great Idea
ENGINEERING

The Chunnel

By Stuart A. Kallen

NORWOOD HOUSE PRESS

Cover: The Chunnel approaches the train terminal in Folkestone, United Kingdom.

Norwood House Press
P.O. Box 316598
Chicago, Illinois 60631

For information regarding Norwood House Press, please visit our Web site at:
www.norwoodhousepress.com or call 866-565-2900.

PHOTO CREDITS: Cover: © Qaphotos.com/Alamy; © AP Images, 13; © AP Images/David Caulkin, 11; © AP Images/Michael Spingler, 41; © AP Images/Odyssey Marine Exploration, Inc., 9; Bow Editorial Services, 14, 18, 23, 28; © David Gee/Alamy, 38; © Gerry Penny/AFP/ Getty Images, 45; © Jacques Langevin/Sygma/Corbis, 17; © Pool Photography/Corbis, 36; © Qaphotos.com/Alamy, 5, 20, 25, 31; © SSPL/Getty Images, 16, 21; © Thibault Camus/AP/Corbis, 39; © Thomas Coex/AFP/Getty Images, 29; © Urban Images/Alamy, 33

LIBRARY OF CONGRESS CATALOGING-IN-PUBLICATION DATA

Kallen, Stuart A., 1955-
  The Chunnel / by Stuart Kallen.
    pages cm. -- (A great idea)
  Summary: "Describes the struggles and accomplishments in building The Chunnel which connects England and France, traveling beneath the English Channel. Includes glossary, websites, and bibliography for further reading"--Provided by publisher.
  Includes index.
  ISBN 978-1-59953-596-8 (library edition : alkaline paper)
  ISBN 978-1-60357-589-8 (ebook)
  1. Channel Tunnel (Coquelles, France, and Folkestone, England)--Juvenile literature. 2. Railroad tunnels--English Channel--Design and construction--Juvenile literature. I. Title.
  TF238.C4K25 2013
  624.1'940916336--dc23
                                                    2013012255

Manufactured in the United States of America in North Mankato, Minnesota.
233N—072013

Contents

Note: Words that are **bolded** in the text are defined in the glossary.

Chapter 1

An Undersea Connection

It was 11:00 a.m. on December 1, 1990. Two men pushed down hard on rattling **jackhammers**. They stood on opposite sides of a 1-foot-thick (30cm), grey rock wall. The man on one side was a British worker named Robert Graham Fagg. On the other side a French worker named Philippe Cozette created dust and din. At twelve minutes past the hour, a small hole opened up between the two men. The jackhammers fell silent. Cozette stuck his right arm through the hole. His left arm and body followed.

The air suddenly pulsed with popping camera flashbulbs. Hundreds of workers, **engineers**, and reporters in hard hats were there. They let out yelps, hoots, and cheers. They were gathered in the middle of a huge tunnel. The tunnel was carved 132 feet (40m) below the English Channel. The Chunnel, also known as the Channel Tunnel or Eurotunnel, stretched 31.3 miles

On December 1, 1990, British construction worker Robert Graham Fagg and Frenchman Philippe Cozette met at the middle of the tunnel.

(50.4km). It was the longest undersea tunnel in the world. As the rock wall fell away, Great Britain and France were linked for the first time since the Ice Age ended around 10,000 years before.

Work continued on the Chunnel for three and a half more years. By May 1994 modern electric trains whisked passengers, vehicles, and cargo through the Chunnel. The trains moved at more than 100 miles per hour (161kph).

By the 2010s more than 9 million people a year were making the 30-minute trip through the Chunnel. While most of them did not think about it, the Chunnel was a big achievement. The project's chief

Passports Stamped

On December 1, 1990, the British news service BBC ran a story on the Chunnel. The story described the first contact between English and French crews digging from opposite sides of the Chunnel:

> Construction workers have drilled through the final wall of rock to join the two halves of the Channel Tunnel and link Britain to France.... To a throng of cheers, construction workers celebrated with champagne—the only time alcohol has been allowed underground on the work site. French worker, Philippe Cozette, and his British counterpart, Graham Fagg, waved flags and shook hands as the first men able to walk between the two countries.... The men continued drilling until a hole was created big enough to allow vehicles through. The first Britons walked through the tunnel to have their passports stamped in France.

engineering director was Gordon Crighton. He said, "You're talking about one of the biggest engineering projects that's ever been built. . . . And yes, even [bigger than] the pyramids."

Wars and Tunnels

People had reason to celebrate the historic Chunnel breakthrough in 1990. The idea of connecting England and France had been a dream for nearly 200 years. Before the Chunnel was built, the only way to travel between the two nations was across the English Channel. The channel's narrowest point is between Calais, France, and Dover, England. There, the sea journey is about 26 miles (42km).

The grey, churning waters of the English Channel are very dangerous. For much of the year the weather is cold. It is also very windy and stormy. Over the centuries hundreds of ships have been wrecked in the channel waters. Thousands of people have died there. But the channel has also acted as a natural barrier between France and Great Britain. The two nations were at war off and on for nearly eight centuries between 1066 and 1815.

Despite the long history of conflict, the first plans for a channel tunnel were made by a French mining engineer in 1802. Albert Mathieu dreamed of building two tunnels. One large tube would be lit by oil lamps. It would be used by horse-drawn carriages. There would be a second, smaller tunnel. It would bring

Did You Know?

The official currency of The United Kingdom is the pound, while, at the time the Chunnel was built, France's currency was the franc, but today is the euro. In this book, all money is expressed in U.S. dollars.

fresh air to passengers below ground. The British government rejected Mathieu's plan. Politicians feared that such a tunnel would give the French an attack route.

Submarine Locomotives

Plans for a link between France and Great Britain went nowhere for decades. But in 1834 a French mining engineer, Aimé Thomé de Gamond, started thinking of

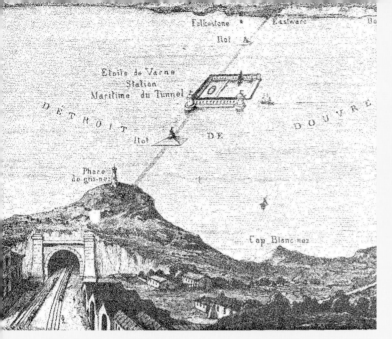

Aimé Thomé de Gamond's plan called for an iron-tube tunnel to be built on the floor of the English Channel.

ways to connect the two nations. Over the next 30 years, he made seven detailed plans for a channel tunnel. One of his ideas was to build iron tubes that would be laid on the seabed. The tubes would hold railroad tracks for the steam locomotives. These were brand-new inventions at the time. Gamond also drew up plans for five different cross-channel bridges. He even had an idea to build huge dams at either end of the channel so it could be drained of all water. None of his plans were ever taken seriously.

Throughout the rest of the 19th century, there were dozens of ideas to link England and France. One idea called for suspended tubes that would swing in the air. Another was for **submerged** roadways under the water. One plan sounded like science fiction. Contractor Alexandre Lavalley proposed building submarine locomotives. These would run on underwater train tracks.

A Chunnel Invitation

By the 1950s France and Great Britain were no longer enemies. The nations had been allies against the Germans in World War I and II. In 1955 the British government finally said it was no longer opposed to a channel tunnel on military grounds. But plans for a cross-channel link were put off for nearly 30 more years. Finally, in 1984 French president François Mitterrand and British prime minister Margaret Thatcher

Channel Shipwrecks

Thousands of sailors and travelers have died in the English Channel over the years. At least 275 ships have gone down in the channel due to storms, rough waters, wars, and piracy. One of the most famous shipwrecks was found in 2008. American salvage divers found the HMS *Victory* in the channel beneath 300 feet (91m) of water.

The ship sank in a storm in 1744. One thousand crew members drowned. The *Victory* was one of the most advanced warships of the day. It had 110 huge cannons made of bronze. Divers compared the ship with a modern aircraft carrier armed with nuclear weapons. The ship was also hauling 3 tons (2.7t) of gold and silver coins for Dutch bankers. The coins are valued today at $1 billion.

In 2008 Odyssey Marine Exploration announced they had discovered the long-lost wreck of the HMS Victory. Here workers recover a 42-pound cannon from the shipwreck.

agreed to build the Chunnel. Neither nation wished to fund such a huge project. So a contest was held.

On April 2, 1985, the French and British issued a 64-page "Invitation to Promoters." This called on private companies to submit plans to design, fund, and build a channel tunnel. The tunnel would have to last at least 120 years. It would also have to resist terrorist attacks and be very safe for travel.

Promoters had to show they could raise huge sums of money. The cost of the project was estimated to be around $3.6 billion. The deadline was short. All plans had to be turned in by October 31, 1985.

Ten plans were turned in to the contest. In his book *The Chunnel*, journalist Drew Fetherston says the plans "ranged from the ridiculous to the barely possible." One plan was for a long suspension bridge partly held in the air by giant helium-filled gasbags. Another plan was called the EuroRoute. This was a road. It would include suspension bridges, ramps, and tunnels. These would be linked to two human-made islands.

Only one plan seemed to make sense and was chosen. It was from Balfour Beatty Construction. The companys' plan was to build three tunnels under the channel. There would be two single-track railway tunnels. These would be 25 feet (7.6m) in **diameter**. They would run parallel, or side by side. They would be 98 feet (30m) apart from each other. A third tunnel would be 16 feet (4.9m) in diameter. It would be a service tunnel with a roadway. It would be used only by emergency and maintenance crews. The service tunnel would also hold utilities. These included drainage pipes, electric wires, and communication cables.

French president François Mitterrand and British prime minister Margaret Thatcher shake hands at the Canterbury Cathedral signing ceremony in 1986 that paved the way for the building and operation of the Chunnel.

The EuroRoute

One of the ideas in 1985 for a cross-channel link was called the EuroRoute. The plan called for a network of tunnels, bridges, roads, ramps, and railroads. The EuroRoute would carry 100,000 cars a day. There would be huge six-lane suspension bridges. These would carry road traffic out about 5 miles (8km) to artificial islands built off the French and British coasts. The islands would have huge spiral ramps like those in parking garages. These ramps would be 820 feet (250m) wide. They would carry traffic up and down from a 12-mile (19km) tunnel in the seabed. A second tunnel under the channel would carry rail traffic. The plan had major backers. These included large banks and British steel companies. But the technology did not exist to build long suspension bridges. Also, the high bridges, spiral ramps, and long tunnel would be a challenge for drivers and might even frighten them. This could create huge traffic jams. The costly plan was finally rejected.

The Chunnel trains would be electric. They would haul people and their cars. Companies could ship cargo on semitrailer trucks loaded on flatbed rail cars.

Channel Tunnel Group

The Chunnel was expected to take seven years to finish. No one knew whether the plan would really work. There were several risks involved in building the tunnel. These included floods, cave-ins, explosions, and fires in tunnels deep under the sea. Workers could lose their lives in accidents. And even if everything went smoothly, the Chunnel might not make money for its backers.

Despite the hurdles, Balfour Beatty teamed up with five banks and nine other companies to build the Chunnel. In July

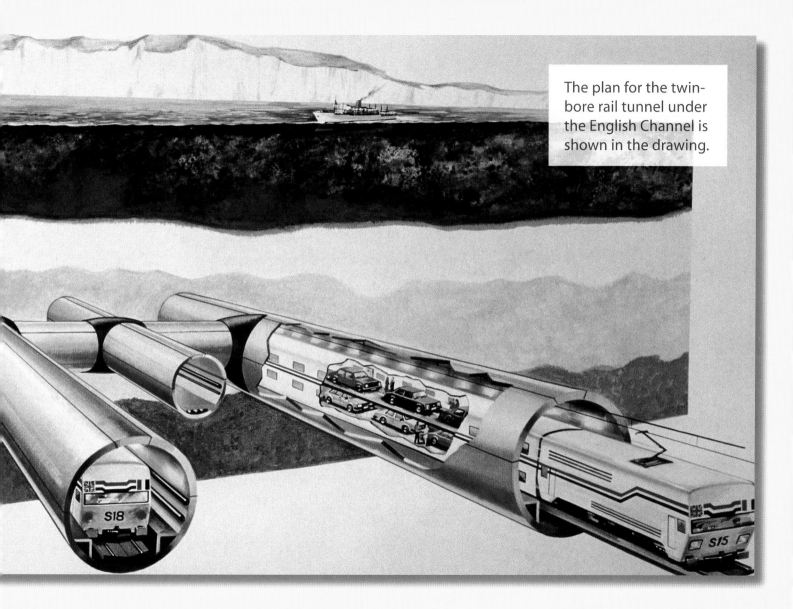

The plan for the twin-bore rail tunnel under the English Channel is shown in the drawing.

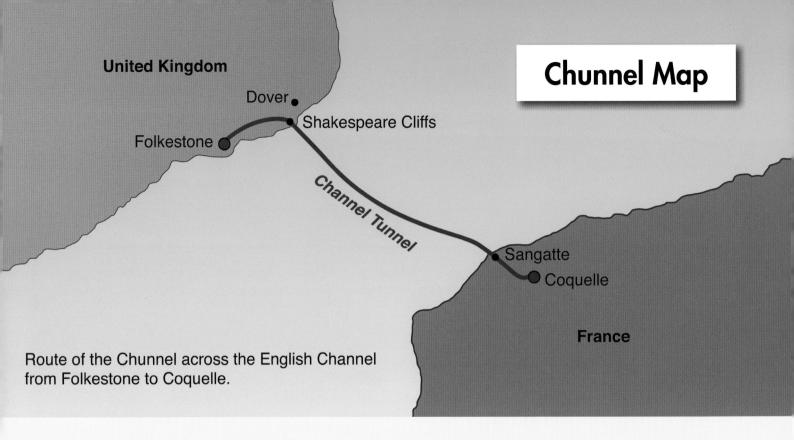

United Kingdom

Dover

Shakespeare Cliffs

Folkestone

Channel Tunnel

Sangatte

Coquelle

France

Route of the Chunnel across the English Channel
from Folkestone to Coquelle.

1985 these groups formed the Channel Tunnel Group/France-Manche or (CTG/F-M). It would take two more years for the British and French to officially approve the project. And it would take until the end of 1987 before ground was broken. By that time the projected cost had already more than doubled. But 185 years after the first plans for a cross-channel link were drawn up, tunneling had begun.

Chapter 2

Tunneling for the Chunnel

By 1987 the Chunnel had come to life on a 250,000-page plan. These plans showed every detail for building a railroad through the world's longest undersea tunnel. There were engineers and designers in 14 different offices in Paris and London. On the English and French coasts, construction managers rounded up equipment. They needed everything from hammers and screwdrivers to massive hole diggers. These were called tunnel boring machines (TBMs). Companies were also hiring a Chunnel workforce. This would swell to 13,000 skilled and

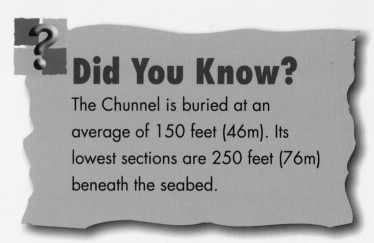

Did You Know?

The Chunnel is buried at an average of 150 feet (46m). Its lowest sections are 250 feet (76m) beneath the seabed.

unskilled workers. These people would work around the clock in three shifts. The digging and building would not stop until the first trains rolled through the Chunnel.

The Tunnel at Shakespeare Cliffs

In December 1987, British workers gathered around a hole beneath Shakespeare Cliffs on the English coast. This was a rural site between Dover and the village of Folkestone. The sea crashed on one side of the hole. Towering white cliffs jutted into the sky on the other side. The workers were about to enter a small, sloping tunnel. It was created in 1974 when the British and French first tried to build a tunnel across the channel.

In December 1987 the British began digging the Chunnel at Shakespeare Cliffs in England.

The earlier effort beneath Shakespeare Cliffs had been called off because the English government decided not to finance the project. But thirteen years later, workers began digging toward France. The old tunnel came to life again. Within weeks, a large vertical shaft was finished.

The shaft was 360 feet (110m) deep. At the bottom a cavern was carved into the rock. The cavern was called a marshaling chamber. The 65-foot-deep (20m) chamber was the main access point for the Chunnel. Workers, materials, and equipment would be gathered there.

The French Side

In June 1988 the French started building their base of operations in Sangatte. This is a small village near Calais. Like the British, the French dug a large vertical shaft to use as a marshaling chamber. It was 180 feet (55m) across and 250 feet

In June 1988 the French built their base of tunnel operations in the small village of Sangatte near Calais.

The Chalky Chunnel

The route of the Chunnel was chosen by **geologists** who studied the rock under the English Channel. They found that the ground was made up of three layers of soft rock called chalk marl. The two upper layers of chalk were porous or permeable. This means water from the channel could easily flow through them and flood the tunnels. The lowest layer of chalk was about 260 feet (80m) thick. It was mixed with clay. Clay is very impermeable, or waterproof. This made the perfect rock for tunneling. It was soft enough to allow English TBMs to dig 985 feet (300m) of tunnel in a week. On the French side, the chalk was more porous and harder to tunnel. The French TBMs moved more slowly. But they managed to meet the British about a third of the way along the Chunnel.

This geological profile of the tunnel shows the many layers of chalk and clay that needed to be bored through by the boring machines.

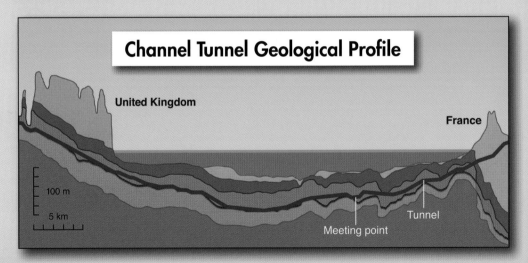

Channel Tunnel Geological Profile

United Kingdom

France

100 m

5 km

Meeting point

Tunnel

(76m) deep. Five elevators were built. Two small elevators could move twelve people each from the surface to the floor of the shaft. Three large elevators were built. These could move 7.5 tons (6.8t) of equipment and building materials, equal to 80 people. The large elevators could also hold a small service train. This was called a "manrider." It was used to take workers into the tunnel. Above the Sangatte shaft, a large hoist called a gantry crane was set in place. This crane could hold 430 tons (390t). It was used to raise and lower equipment into the shaft.

While the chambers were being built, workers on both sides built cement factories. These would make the thick concrete liners for the walls of the Chunnel. Workers also built power plants and loading docks. And they built repair facilities for trains, vehicles, and machines.

Tunnel Boring Machines

The most important piece of Chunnel building equipment was lowered into the chambers piece by piece. TBMs are huge machines. They are designed to cut through solid rock. Eleven TBMs were made for digging the Chunnel by the Robbins Company of Seattle, Washington. Six were put together in the English marshaling chamber and five in the French. Each TBM was designed to dig out one of the three tunnels. Three would work from the English side, three from the French side. The others were on call as backup machines.

The TBMs were engineering marvels on their own. Each one weighed 15,000

Workers assemble one of the eleven huge tunnel boring machines that would be used to excavate the tunnel.

a cutter head. The cutters carved round holes into the chalk and clay soil. The electric-powered cutters were 14 to 28 feet (4.3m to 8.5m) in diameter. They chewed through the rock with teeth made from tungsten carbide. This is three times harder than steel. Each machine could bore about 750 feet (229m) of tunnel a day. During every hour of operation, a TBM produced about 24,000 tons (21,772t) of debris called spoil.

On the English side, the spoil was moved away on conveyer belts. It was dumped into railroad cars called muck wagons and carried to the surface. On the French side, the spoil was crushed and mixed with water. This formed a liquid called slurry, which was as thick as yogurt. It was pumped out of the tunnel by six

tons (13,608t) and was 750 feet (229m) long. They stretched the length of two soccer fields or two and a half football fields. At the front of each machine was slurry pumps. Each pump drained enough slurry every hour to cover a baseball diamond to a depth of nearly 40 feet (12m). The slurry was stored in a large natural basin called Fond Pignon. Over time the water drained away and the crushed rock remained. It eventually hardened into a chalky rock layer 131 feet (40m) thick.

Hard, Hot Work

The people who built the Chunnel worked in a hot, harsh underground world. Water was constantly sprayed around the TBMs to keep the dust down. This raised the humidity in the Chunnel to nearly 100 percent. That is equal to a tropical jungle. The machines also put out a lot of heat. Temperatures below ground were around 100°F (38°C). Workers sweated constantly. Their clothes stayed drenched. During an eight-hour shift, the average worker drank 1.5 gallons (5.7L) of water. The heat was only part of the hardship. Much digging was done by hand with jackhammers. And many parts of the Chunnel were dim and confining. In these harsh conditions some workers only lasted several hours before quitting.

Workers had to endure temperatures below ground of 100 °F (38°C) due to the heat generated by the boring machines.

"Groping for a Pinpoint"

TBMs are loud, earthshaking, power-sucking monsters that cut through solid rock. They could only move forward. After digging millions of tons of dirt, they still had another hard goal. The TBM from England had to meet up with the TBM from France. The two tunnels, coming from opposite directions, could not be more than 8.2 feet (2.5m) out of line.

High-speed train tracks have to follow a fairly straight path. There could be no kinks or turns in the 23.5-mile (38km) section of the tunnel under the seabed. If the machines failed to meet, the project would have to be scrapped or restarted. Either way tens of millions of dollars would be lost. As Drew Fetherston says in *The Chunnel*, the TBMs were "groping for a pinpoint."

Laser Guidance

During most of 1988 French and British teams worked toward each other in the service tunnel. The TBM operators used the most advanced satellite mapping equipment of the day to keep the machines on course. Engineers also used a laser guidance system. A drill bit 2.5

The Tunnels in the Chunnel

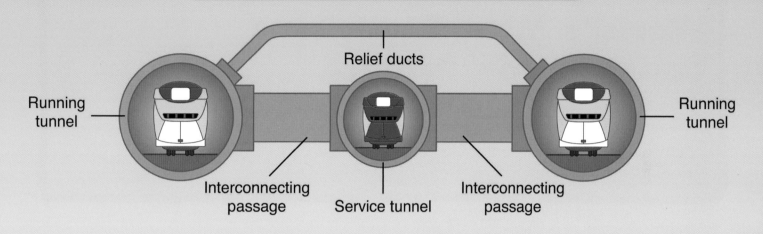

A crosscut diagram of the Channel Tunnel

inches (6.4cm) wide was attached to the front of the TBM. This drilled a small hole, which sent a red laser light forward. Engineers programmed the laser guidance system to follow an exact path which was stored on computers in the operator's cabin. The computer calculated the actual location of the laser beam and compared it with the desired path. If the actual path of the TBM did not match the path engineers wanted, the TBM driver could made adjustments to

World's Most Expensive Construction Project

The Chunnel project faced many setbacks. Eleven workers were killed. There were fires, floods, and equipment failures. In addition, there were money problems from start to finish. The project was expected to cost $3.6 billion. By 1993 the price had grown to $14 billion. By the time the project was finished, the cost was $21 billion. This made the Chunnel the costliest construction project in history.

steer the machine on the proper path as it chewed through the earth.

Huge concrete rings equal to the diameter of the tunnel were bolted into the walls behind the TBMs. The concrete was reinforced with steel bars. This would help the tunnel withstand the pressure bearing down on it from the water above. The concrete was stronger than the walls of nuclear power plants.

By 1989 the Chunnel project was almost a year behind schedule. Costs were climbing rapidly. On January 20 the first tragedy occurred on the English side. Andrew McKenna was a nineteen-year-old engineering assistant. He died after he was struck by a service train loaded with spoil.

McKenna's was the first death. But it was not the last. Before the Chunnel was finished, 11 workers would die in accidents.

The Final Connection

On October 30, 1990, the French and British TBMs were separated by less than 100 feet (30.5m) of earth between the two tunnels. The British drilled a long hole by hand. A thin rod was threaded through the drill hole. The probe broke through on the French side as workers cheered. The two sides were only off course by about 20 inches (51cm). The engineers could easily fix this. The mission was a success. It would take another month before the official breakthrough. On December 1, 1990, Chunnel workers Robert Graham Fagg and Philippe Cozette shook hands as the cameras rolled.

After the celebration died down, Chunnel engineers had a huge problem: TBMs cannot go in reverse. The two monsters were face to face deep under the English

Workers from France and Great Britain celebrate the meeting of the borers that completed the first tunnel.

Channel. Planners at first proposed taking the huge machines apart. Pieces would be carted out on trains. But this would be costly and very time consuming.

The engineers made new plans on the spot. The English TBM was turned into the side of the tunnel. It was driven forward until it was buried in the rock. The hole was sealed, and the wall was covered with a concrete slab. That machine remains there today, sacrificed after performing one of the most amazing tunneling jobs in history. The French TBM, Brigitte, was driven forward and out to the English coast.

TBMs Shut Off

After the breakthrough in the service tunnel, workers had to dig two more tunnels for the trains. These were nearly twice as wide as the service tunnel. On May 22, 1991, two TBMs met again in the north train tunnel. About five weeks later, on June 28, the TBMs were face to face in the south tunnel. In both cases, one TBM was buried in the wall so the other could be driven out of the hole. After four years of digging, the tunnels were complete.

By the time the digging phase was over, workers had dug about 90 miles (145km) of tunnel. They removed enough spoil to cover 80 acres (32ha). That is equal to 68 football fields. Some of the workers had been working in the dark, damp, noisy tunnels six days a week for years. When the last tunnel was complete, the TBMs were shut off. As their roars died down, quiet fell in the Chunnel for the first time.

Chapter 3

Rolling on the Railroad

The three channel tunnels that link England and France were finished in 1991. It would take three more years to finish the Chunnel operating systems. These were known as **infrastructure**. The finished concrete tubes needed special tracks for high-speed trains. Complex signal, lighting, ventilation, security, and emergency systems needed to be set up. Passenger depots had to be built at both ends. These would need parking lots, loading docks, public transportation links, and shipping terminals. Rail connections had to be linked to Europe's main lines. And the trains had to be specially built and designed to whoosh through the Chunnel at speeds of 100 miles per hour (161kph). Outside the Chunnel the trains would travel at 168 miles per hour (270kph).

Before the tracks were laid, workers had to carve out two huge rooms under the sea. These rooms were called crossover links.

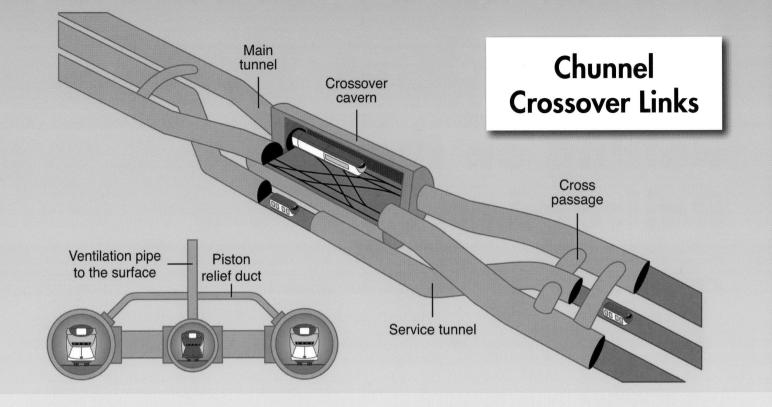

Chunnel Crossover Links

Main tunnel

Crossover cavern

Cross passage

Ventilation pipe to the surface

Piston relief duct

Service tunnel

They joined the rail tunnels. The links would let a train switch from one set of tracks to the other. Switching might be needed when maintenance work was being done in one of the tunnels. The links would also be used in emergencies. Stranded passengers could move through the links to a rescue train. During normal operations, giant steel doors moved by motors closed off the crossover links.

Like everything else about the Chunnel, the concrete-lined crossover links are huge. They are 40 feet (12m) tall and 500 feet (152m) long. The links are the largest undersea caverns ever made. Workers nicknamed the rooms"cathedrals."

Air Pressure

More digging was needed to build what are called piston relief ducts. These tube-shaped passages were cut by workers with

Emergency Systems

The operating systems of the Chunnel were designed to handle emergencies such as fires, explosions, and train derailments. The systems are based around two large shafts at each end of the Chunnel. They are run by control centers in Shakespeare Cliffs and Calais. Each shaft gives emergency crews access to the three tunnels. A large reservoir holds water for firefighting. Huge diesel generators make electricity for trains. They also provide lighting during power failures. A vent system is used only for emergencies. Two powerful fans are connected to a duct system in the rail tunnels. The fans are reversible. They can suck fumes and smoke out of the tunnel in case of fire. They can also bring fresh air to any areas where people might be stranded.

French firemen participate in a firefighting drill in the Chunnel. Chunnel emergency systems handle fires, explosions, and train derailments.

jackhammers. Piston relief ducts are located every 820 feet (250m). They connect the two railway tunnels. The ducts are reinforced with cast-iron segments. They arch over the service tunnel in the middle.

Piston relief valves are needed because high-speed trains push a lot of air. This makes a strong wind in the tunnel called air pressure. The piston relief ducts allow the air pressure to flow into the other train tunnel. When trains pass each other in their separate tunnels, the valves close. This prevents huge blasts of air from affecting passing trains.

Workers also used their jackhammers to carve out more tunnels and caverns. These were for control rooms, utility substations, and emergency pumping stations. Narrow walkways were put in for workers and passengers to use in emergencies.

Electric Locomotives

As the last Chunnel work was being finished, factories in Europe were making train vehicles. These were known as rolling stock. The rolling stock included locomotives, passenger coaches, vehicle wagons, and freight cars.

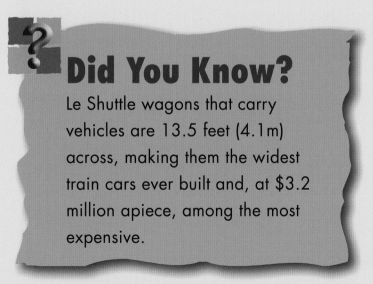

Did You Know?

Le Shuttle wagons that carry vehicles are 13.5 feet (4.1m) across, making them the widest train cars ever built and, at $3.2 million apiece, among the most expensive.

Designed to pull 20 rail cars, the Chunnel uses 34 locomotives for 17 shuttles to move people and goods across the channel.

The train service between Folkestone and Calais is called Le Shuttle. The system uses nine rail cars. These move people and their cars through the Chunnel by rail. Eight more large vehicle wagons are used to move large trucks by rail through the Chunnel. Each Le Shuttle train is driven by 2 locomotives. A total of 34 locomotives were needed for the 17 Le Shuttle trains. The trains can pull 20 rail cars. This made them the longest passenger trains in the world.

Each locomotive weighs about 25 tons (22.7t). It has 12 wheels attached to six axles. Electric engines power the axles and drive the train. The electricity is brought to the locomotive by a high-voltage contact wire that runs overhead.

The locomotives had to be designed to meet the challenges of Chunnel travel. Each Le Shuttle train had locomotives at the front and back of the cars. If the front engine broke down, the back locomotive could push the train out of the Chunnel.

Cold and Hot

The electric locomotives would make 20 trips a day. The engines had to be very strong. They had to be able to pull 2,700 tons (2,500t) up the steep grades at the ends of the Chunnel. The trains also had to deal with sudden, drastic changes in temperature. Outdoor winter temperatures were often below freezing at ground level. They were over 100°F (38°C) inside the Chunnel.

Signal Systems

The Chunnel was designed to allow two trains to run at 100 mph (161kph) only three minutes apart. This could only work with a very advanced signal system. When trains run, they send out an electrical signal through the wheels and rails. These signals give the exact location of each train to a computer in the rail control center in Folkestone. The computers regulate the speed of each train. The trains are slowed, stopped, or sped up depending on conditions. Operators can see the location and movement of each train on a computer screen. The system is built with multiple computers. These are on standby in case anything happens to the one in use.

Heat in the Chunnel proved to be a big challenge in other ways. During early test runs, temperatures under the locomotives reached 140°F (60°C). This heat created a fire danger. Designers were called on to solve this problem as quickly as possible. They came up with a giant air-conditioning system. A cold-water pipeline was installed along the Chunnel tracks to absorb heat. The heated water was pumped out to cooling stations built at either end. The water was then chilled and sent back through the system.

Rolling Wagons

Le Shuttle has other unique rolling stock in addition to locomotives. The wagons that carry cars and trucks are the largest railway vehicles in the world. There are two types. Double-decker wagons can carry a total of 10 passenger cars. Single-deck wagons carry trailers, vans, SUVs, and other tall vehicles. Both types of wagon are 85 feet (26m) long and weigh 71 tons (64t). The wagons are made from stainless steel. They are insulated with fire-resistant materials. Passengers drive their vehicles directly on and off the wagons.

There are two types of wagons that carry cars and trucks. Double-decker wagons are designed to carry 10 passenger cars each.

Each wagon has a long, flat floor with side curbs. It has a special place for motorcycles.

Freight shuttle wagons were designed to carry semitrailers. The British call the trailers lorries. The freight wagons are partly open. They have a cage-like structure that surrounds each lorry. Sunken sections with drainage equipment collect any leaking oil which is later thrown away.

First Run

Six years and one week after the first hole was bored under Shakespeare Cliffs, the rolling stock was in place. The tracks, signals, and other infrastructure were

The Terminals

While the Chunnel was being built, brand-new train terminals were built at Folkestone and near Calais. The terminals were designed to move passengers, cars, and trucks onto Le Shuttle trains. They also provide airport-type services. These include passenger handling, catering, administration, customs, and immigration. Like the Chunnel, the terminals are engineering wonders. The Calais terminal holds eight concrete island platforms between sets of train tracks. Cars and trucks drive down ramps, where they are loaded onto rail cars. The passenger terminal is located at the end of a loop of train tracks. This loop lets the locomotives turn around for the journey back into the Chunnel.

complete. On December 10, 1993, all work was done. It was time for private celebrations on both sides of the Chunnel. Invitations were sent to many people. These included politicians who backed the project, bankers who funded it, engineers who designed it, and workers who built it. In terminals on both sides, waiters served food and champagne. Around 3:30 p.m. the first train carrying passengers left the Calais terminal. It gathered speed and moved down into the chalky depths beneath the channel.

Little more than 35 minutes later, the train glided into Folkestone. Another train filled with English passengers soon entered the Chunnel. It headed to France. The passengers celebrated, but there wasn't much to see along the way. As Drew Fetherston notes in *The Chunnel*, "All the wealth of

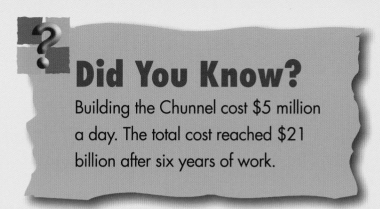

Did You Know?

Building the Chunnel cost $5 million a day. The total cost reached $21 billion after six years of work.

detail that had absorbed the thoughts and labors of thousands of men and women— the cross-passages, the chiller pipes, the piston relief ducts—flickered by too rapidly for the eye to grasp. . . . Mile after mile of wall flew by the windows."

The Queen and the President

The official public opening of the Chunnel took place on May 6, 1994. England's Queen Elizabeth and France's

On May 6, 1994, President François Mitterrand and Queen Elizabeth cut the ribbons to officially open the Chunnel.

François Mitterrand were the first to travel. The queen headed to France on one train while Mitterrand traveled toward England on another. The two trains met nose-to-nose in the middle of the Chunnel. (The computer system that prevents two trains from traveling on the same track was turned off for the event.) The queen and the president cut red, white, and blue ribbons. The French and English national anthems were played. The queen called the project "one of the world's great technological achievements."

The Chunnel was certainly a great engineering feat. But on that day in May, the future of Le Shuttle was uncertain. The project cost billions to build. No one knew whether it would ever pay for itself. Whatever the case, the Chunnel was finished. What had been a dream for nearly 200 years was now a reality.

Chapter 4

Historic Link

In July 1994 the Chunnel was opened to the public. The world's longest undersea tunnel was considered one of the seven wonders of the modern world. This created a lot of interest and instantly attracted passengers. The trip not only held the novelty of crossing under the English Channel. It was also quick. The 30-minute journey was twice as fast as the quickest ferries. And no one ever got seasick or shipwrecked traveling through the Chunnel.

Passengers have two options for traveling through the Chunnel. Le Shuttle lets people drive their cars right onto train wagons. Passengers can stay in their cars for the trip, or they can walk around the vehicle wagon. It takes about 30 minutes to load all the cars onto the trains and another 30 minutes for them to drive off. One-way tickets are around $25.

Travelers without cars can take high-speed trains on the Eurostar line. These

Travelers without cars can take high-speed trains and travel between London and Paris in about two and a half hours.

travel between London and Paris through the Chunnel. They also travel between London and Brussels, Belgium. Either trip lasts about about two and a half hours.

Flames Under a Truck

By 1996 about 70 percent of all travelers between England and France rode on Eurostar trains or Le Shuttle. And about 40 percent of all commercial trucks used the Chunnel. The future looked promising. Then disaster struck.

It happened around 9:45 p.m. on November 18, 1996. A freight shuttle was moving 29 trucks from Calais to Folkestone. As the train moved into the South Tunnel, several security guards noticed a fire under one of the trucks near the middle of the rail wagon. Flames rose more than 6 feet (1.8m) into the air.

It took about 10 minutes for word of the fire to reach the rail control center in Folkestone. By that time the train was cruising through the Chunnel at nearly

? Did You Know?

Passenger vehicles and freight vehicles are carried on separate Le Shuttle trains.

The burnt remains of a truck are seen being pulled out of the Chunnel after a fire on November 18, 1996. No one was injured.

90 mph (145kph). A fire-detection system sent an emergency signal to the train engineer. Four fire alarms clanged loudly in the Chunnel. The engineer was told to take the train to an emergency rail siding on the English side of the Chunnel.

For the first time Chunnel emergency plans were put into place. The piston relief ducts were closed to prevent smoke from spreading. Despite these efforts, a train in the North Tunnel was engulfed with smoke. Five other trains in the tunnels were slowed to about 62 mph (100kph). Other trains were prevented from entering the Chunnel.

Fire in the Hole

The troubled train was proceeding as instructed. The engineers soon learned the stricken rail wagon was tilting at a dangerous angle. There were fears that this might cause the train to fall off the tracks, or derail. The driver's control board lit up with an emergency stop light. The train stopped at a crossover link. When it stopped, toxic black smoke surged forward and enveloped the train. The smoke began to seep into the passenger coach, where 31 people were riding behind the locomotive. They were stranded about 12 miles (19km) from

? Did You Know?
Between 1994 and 2012 more than 265 million people had made the Chunnel journey, along with 17 million trucks.

Trapped Beneath the Chunnel

On December 18, 2009, a record-setting snowstorm hit Great Britain and northern France. That night five Eurostar trains carrying 2,000 people ground to a halt in the middle of the Chunnel. The travelers were trapped overnight. They had no lights, power, food, water, or bathrooms. It was freezing outdoors. But temperatures in the Chunnel reached about 104°F (40°C). The air-conditioning systems were not working. Some passengers fainted or got very ill.

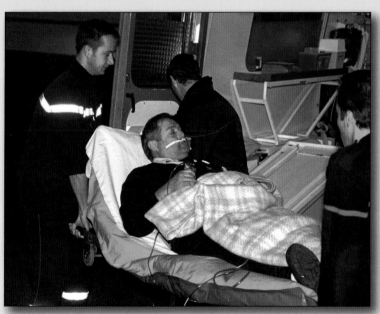

The problems were caused by huge chunks of snow that piled up on the trains aboveground. When the trains entered the warm Chunnel, the snow melted off. This caused the electric system to short-circuit. Eventually, 1,365 people had to walk to safety while another 635 had to be rescued with emergency vehicles. The stranded travelers were offered a full refund and about $200 for their troubles.

An injured man is carried by rescue workers to safety after a fire broke out in the Chunnel. Two thousand passengers were trapped overnight in the tunnels.

the French terminal and 20 miles (32km) from the English terminal.

The conductor of the stranded train opened the doors to the passenger car to lead the travelers to safety. Smoke rushed in, forcing passengers to lie on the floor. There was panic as people began to choke.

Emergency fans were turned on to blow fresh air into the tunnel. But due to an operating error, it took about 20 minutes for fresh air to reach the area. And the fans made the situation worse. The fire had been growing slowly under one of the trucks. The rush of fresh air fanned the flames. The fire got bigger.

Chunnel Refugees

Beginning in 1997 the Chunnel provided a new kind of historic link. Thousands of refugees were trying to enter England illegally through the Chunnel. The refugees were from Afghanistan, Africa, and elsewhere. They wanted to get into England because it was easier to get jobs there. By the late 1990s hundreds of immigrants every night were trying to stow away on Le Shuttle. Some jumped from bridges onto rolling wagons that hauled semitrailer trucks. Others gathered in groups and entered the Chunnel on foot. Some walked several miles before authorities stopped them.

In 1999, so many people were trying to sneak through the Chunnel that the Red Cross opened a refugee camp near the tunnel entrance, in Sangatte, France. By 2001 more than 1,200 asylum seekers were living in the Red Cross camp. About 400 were trying to stow away each night, and at least a dozen died. The camp was shut down in 2002. In the years that followed, increased security was put in place, and the Chunnel was no longer used as an illegal port of entry.

The fans cleared the smoke enough for emergency crews to lead passengers safely to a service tunnel. Meanwhile, firefighters had to deal with the burning truck that had started the fire. It was carrying 22 tons (20t) of flammable animal fat. Several explosions rocked the Chunnel as the fat burned.

About one hour after the train entered the tunnel, passengers were loaded onto another train running north. They arrived back in France within half an hour. They were taken to hospitals for treatment of minor injuries. The fire was finally put out at five o'clock the next morning.

There was a great deal of fire damage to the Chunnel. Temperatures had reached more than 2,400°F (1,316°C). This was hot enough turn tracks, wires, pipes, and even the concrete walls into melted, twisted wreckage. About 1,650 feet (503m) of track had to be rebuilt. Nearly 1 mile (1.5km) of signal systems and electrical lines had to be replaced. Fifteen shuttle wagons were damaged. So was the rear locomotive. Ten wagons were completely destroyed. But these were towed from the Chunnel on their own wheels. Luckily all the safety systems had worked, and there were no deaths.

It cost more than $80 million to repair the Chunnel and replace the rolling stock. It took 140 workers more than six months to repair the damage. During this time, trains continued to roll through the North Tunnel, which had not been damaged.

Green Energy

Chunnel trains use a lot of electricity. But in 2012 the Chunnel was the most energy-efficient way for people and goods to cross between England and France. This was due to wind turbines on both sides. These make renewable power for trains and terminals. The Chunnel is also a very low producer of carbon emissions. These emissions add to global warming. A semitrailer crossing the Chunnel produces twenty times less carbon emissions that a ferry crossing. To show off its green energy use, the Chunnel added a carbon counter to its website. This helps people see the savings made on a journey by shuttle compared to travel by ferry.

A Unique Project

The 1996 fire was the worst of several that broke out over the years. There were also fires in August 2006 and September 2008. Both started on rail cars hauling lorries. As with the first fire, there were no serious injuries. There were also a number of train breakdowns. These stranded people for several hours beneath the channel. And during the late 1990s, immigrants began to use the Chunnel to illegally enter England from France.

Fires and train failures were sure to make the news. But problems were rare. In the 2010s nearly 10 million people a year traveled safely through the Chunnel. By 2012 more than 265 million people had made the journey, along with 17 million lorries. A pet shuttle service started in 2000. Since then more than 600,000 dogs and cats have made the trip.

Since a pet shuttle service was started in 2000, more than 600,000 dogs and cats have made the trip under the channel.

In 2010 wind farms were built in France to supply renewable power to the trains. And the Chunnel remains a unique project. It is a historic link. It is also an engineering achievement unlike any other on earth.

diameter [die-AM-eh-ter]: A line through the center of a circle. A tunnel 25 feet (7.6m) in diameter is 25 feet (7.6m) across at its largest width.

engineer [in-jin-EAR]: A person who solves technical and building problems through the use of design, science, math, knowledge of materials, and creativity.

geologist [gee-ALL-uh-jist]: A scientist who studies the rocks and other matter that make up the earth. During Chunnel construction, geologists played an important role in mapping the tunnels through the rock, clay, and chalk under the English Channel.

infrastructure [IN-fra-struck-shur]: Road and railway operating networks that include tunnels, tracks, sewers, electrical systems, terminals, signals, lighting, emergency systems, and ventilation.

jackhammer [JACK-ham-er]: Called a pneumatic drill in Great Britain, this noisy tool combines a hammer with a chisel to break up rock and concrete. Most are powered with compressed air, but some use electric motors.

submerged [sub-MERGED]: Underwater.

For More Information

Books

Brian Floca, *Locomotive*. New York: Atheneum Books for Young Readers, 2013.

Lee Sullivan Hill, *Trains on the Move*. Minneapolis: Lerner, 2012.

Donna Latham, *Bridges and Tunnels: Investigate Feats of Engineering with 25 Projects*. White River Junction, VT: Nomad, 2012.

Susan K. Mitchell, *Mega Structures: The Longest Tunnels*. Portland, OR: ReadHowYouWant, 2012.

Liz Sonneborn, *France*. Danbury, CT: Children's Press, 2013.

Claire Thorpe, *England*. Mankato, MN: Raintree Paperbacks, 2012.

Websites

Discovery, Tunnel Boring Machines http://dsc.discovery.com/tv-shows/other-shows/videos/mega-engineering-tunnel-boring-machines.htm.

Eurotunnel www.eurotunnel.com/build

EuroTunnel Group www.eurotunnel-group.com/uk/the-channel-tunnel

Index

About the Author

Stuart A. Kallen is the author of more than 250 books for children and young adults. His titles have covered history, engineering marvels, art, music, magical mysteries, and folklore. Kallen lives in San Diego, where he hikes, bikes, and plays music in his spare time.